Plainsongs

Plainsongs

Fall 2025

Editor
Eric R. Tucker

Associate Editors
Becky Faber, Michael Catherwood, Eleanor Reeds

Editors Emeriti
Dwight Marsh, Laura Marvel-Wunderlich

Production Assistant
Joaquin Gutierrez

Cover Image
Elizabeth Lowe

Corpus Callosum Press LLC
Hastings, Nebraska

Cover photo by Elizabeth Lowe. Typography and book design by Corpus Callosum Press LLC, Hastings, Nebraska.

Plainsongs is indexed by Humanities International Complete, EBSCO Information Services, 10 Estes Street, Ipswich, MA 01938.

ISBN-13 979-8-9928127-4-9
ISSN 1534-3820

Plainsongs

Winner of the Jane Geske Award,
presented by the Nebraska Center for the Book

Contents

Notes from the Editor

Thank you for picking up issue 1 of volume 44 of *Plainsongs* poetry journal. It is good to be back, and our return to annual publication would not have been possible without the hard work and support of our three dedicated associate editors: Becky Faber, Michael Catherwood, and Eleanor Reeds. We remain so grateful for their invaluable contributions to the journal.

In this issue you will find award-winning poems by Christopher Stewart, Lucy Adkins, and Brandon Kilbourne, award essays written by our associate editors (who were also kind enough to contribute poems of their own), and a beautiful cover image by the filmmaker, photographer, and writer Elizabeth Lowe. All told, this issue contains over seventy poems by talented writers from across the U.S. and around the world.

In these troubling times, poetry can nourish us in so many ways. It asks us to slow down, to pay closer attention. It shakes us awake. It lets us dream. It whispers. It roars. It grieves. It breathes. It ponders. It protests. Sometimes, it screams.

And always, *always*—in a rising collective vocalization, in a resounding chorus that carries across canyon and plain and forest and mountaintop, by a multitude of voices representing the wondrous diversity of humanity, in language that hums with compassion, with empathy, with hope and humility and boundless love—it *sings*.

Thank you for reading.

Eric R. Tucker
Hastings, Nebraska

Goodwill

At the loading dock of the Goodwill,
me and a store manager help a woman
heft a shabby couch into her minivan
which is stuffed with clothes, canned food,
kitchen goods. *It was all in bags,* she roared,
until my motherfucking husband tore them up.
On the other side of a tangle of blue jeans
and frayed towels, I see a toddler's seat.
It's one of those March days
in the liminal space between winter
and spring. The air is thin and dry,
like memories posted in a scrapbook
forgotten in a bureau drawer, and I am
with my mother at the Thrift and Save
on West Roscoe Avenue. She is flipping
through a rack of boys' dress shirts
while two gothy-looking teenagers
give us pitying looks. The blood rises up
the back of my neck. There was nowhere
to put that shame, least that I knew then.
I didn't know it could be a howl, a flaring,
full-throated scream, the peeling of tires
as she tears out of the Goodwill parking lot.

Christopher Stewart
Urbana, Illinois

About "Goodwill": A *Plainsongs* Award Poem

Richard Hugo wrote in *The Triggering Town*, "You are someone and you have a right to your life." Hugo also writes about how Theodore Roethke, a professor of Hugo's, would tell students to take uncomfortable risks in their poetry. By this, he did not mean exotic spelling or awkward line breaks, but that poets armed with their lives would bring energy to subjects.

Christopher Stewart's "Goodwill" takes this advice, maybe unknowingly, but perhaps instinctively. The strength of Stewart's "Goodwill" is to let the poem unfold organically, to detail the scene, create action, and allow characters to speak. All this with great splashes of sensory description.

"Goodwill" is a poem of things, naturally. People go to the Goodwill to find deals, but mostly to find what they need in their lives. Stewart's beginning list is brilliant: *loading dock, shabby couch, bags, frayed towels, husband, canned food,* and *toddler's seat.*

The speaker then shifts to the weather, where "The air is thin and dry, / like memories posted in a scrapbook." This shift reflects the speaker's emotional escape after the lady "roared, /… my motherfucking husband tore them (bags) up." The shifts in time forward and backward are smooth and revealing: "I am / with my mother at the Thrift and Save / on West Roscoe Avenue."

Stewart juggles emotional shifts with the speaker and others in the poem: generosity, kindness, shame, and anger. All these touches help point us to the last lines in the poem, where the experience floods the speaker, proclaiming, "There was nowhere / to put that shame, least that I knew then."

The poem reaches its crescendo with "the peeling of tires / as she tears out of the Goodwill parking lot."

Stewart's "Goodwill" is a strong poem that does not pull back. Readers are quickly immersed in the action and emotion, and with Stewart's fine touch, the poem will not let us look away.

Michael Catherwood
Omaha, Nebraska

My Father, Before the War

In the photograph he is posing
before an ancient car with his friends,
all of them young, seventeen or eighteen,
dressed in suits and hats, fedoras,
and they stand with their hips cocked,
their fedoras slanted, my father with
his foot back against the running board
of the car, which is a Pontiac,
a Ford, a Mercury Club Coupe.
I do not know what kind it is.
It is 1940 or 1941, just before the war,
and they are still immortal,
clowning a little before they board
the train to Omaha for their
draft physicals. How handsome
my father is, dashing, I might say,
his smile a light in him, his forehead
without the furrows he wore
when I knew him, the furrows he plowed
deeper, all the years that came after.

Lucy Adkins
Lincoln, Nebraska

About "My Father, Before the War": A *Plainsongs* Award Poem

In 1914, near the beginning of World War I, August Sander, a German photographer, took a photo of three well-dressed young men. Entitled "Young Farmers," the photograph came to be known as "Three Farmers on Their Way to a Dance." This was the image that came to mind as I began reading "My Father, Before the War."

Lucy Adkins poses her young men casually in front of a car, well dressed and on their way somewhere. Then she drops the harsh clue that changes the entire scope of the poem—"It is 1940 or 1941, just before the war,/and they are still immortal...." Those two lines change the focus of the poem from fun to foxholes. They are not on their way to merriment, but to the medical physical that will determine if they are fit for military service.

I was especially drawn to Adkins' point that she didn't know her father when he was young and without the permanent mark of the war. This is a universal truth—that we have no real way to know our parents when they were youthful. His post-war furrows indicate that war has left its mark on him, changing him from the young man in the photograph. This poem speaks to many of us who have seen such furrows.

Photographs and poetry make us immortal.

Becky Faber
Lincoln, Nebraska

How I Find Dancing with You

Despite my years in biology, even when you do not wear
the leopard rosettes of your long side-split skirt or sport
the zebra stripes of your sleeveless top, you captivate me more
than any overgrown cat or patterned horse no matter how rare,
and certainly, when I dance salsa with you, your movements
are the envy of all antelopes and any creature with a claim to grace
or rhythm, but perhaps this is all moot, as all animals go extinct
in my head when I'm entranced by your eyes as together
we circle to Alexander Abreu and the rhythm of *uno*, *dos*, *tres*, —,
cinco, *seis*, *siete*, —, with everyone else on the dancefloor
disappearing, save for when I need to avoid twirling you
into some body that is not you, because your smile's witchery
reduces seven continents adrift amid five oceans to the area
traversed by our four feet, a spell cast which in turns leads,
despite the high points of moonlight, waterfalls, and platypuses
not to mention board games, chickpeas, and the wonder
that were the vegan donuts that we dined on tonight before dancing,
to a breakthrough understanding that the whole of time's passage
ever since all of existence was spat out by some primordial bang
has been solely to orchestrate this moment revolving around
your face sapphire in the nightclub's blue lights, laughter
released by your lips to lure its mate from my mouth, the North
Star's glint borrowed by a beaded nose ring and fine lines
raying from eye's corner to cross temple, a sight only second
to your speechless gaze when I told you that I see in you
the kindness you admire most about your mother; however,
perhaps all this is just to say that when I'm dancing with you,
I lose myself in the awe and discoveries found no further than
your whorled fingertips, their electric friction with my own
holding, for the length of a song, a two-person world together.

Brandon Kilbourne
Berlin, Germany

About "How I Find Dancing with You": A *Plainsongs* Award Poem

My favorite love poem has always been Frank O'Hara's "Having a Coke with You" and so I was thrilled to discover in this issue Brandon Kilbourne's equally hyperbolic and breathless ode to a lover whose smile "reduces seven continents adrift amid five oceans to the area / traversed by our four feet." Not only space but time, "ever since all of existence was spat out," is subsumed by the experience of dancing "for the length of a song" with a woman who exceeds all possible comparisons in her "grace." In contrast to the "leopard rosettes" and "zebra stripes" of her wardrobe, the majesty of real animals in the wild is radically diminished: such a creature is merely an "overgrown cat or patterned horse" to the speaker "entranced" by their partner. Such bathos reinforces the way in which everyone in physical proximity to the couple is "disappearing" when the speaker can only define another person as "some body that is not you." Just as the extraordinary becomes ordinary in the lover's presence, so does the reverse: "board games, chickpeas, and … vegan donuts" become as much a source of romantic "wonder" as "moonlight, waterfalls, and platypuses."

While O'Hara, a longtime curator at the Museum of Modern Art in New York City, portrayed his lover as exceeding the totality of figurative art, Kilbourne's speaker transforms the biological expertise announced in the poem's opening line into the means to elevate their beloved above all else. Across a teasing line break, the speaker's assertion that "all animals go extinct" is qualified as an effect of their absorption in the beloved, a cataclysmic event that—it turns out—happens "in my head." All possible beauty in the cosmos is "moot" when even the lover's nose ring is able to "borrow… the North / Star's glint." The speaker declares what can be discovered in a moment of intimacy, how one might "Find Dancing with You," in a single sentence unfolding across thirty lines of verse as they attempt to put a sublime experience into inadequate language, repeatedly correcting and hedging. After all, "perhaps all this is just to say that when I'm dancing with you, / I lose myself."

What is "found" in this complete surrender to another is a "two-person world" sustained by the "electric friction" between "fingertips." Carried along by the salsa beat, the reader too is swept up in the epic version of this everyday romance to which even Biblical assertions of love—note the dismissal of the antelope from the Songs of Songs—cannot do justice. "How I Find Dancing with You" narrates a "breakthrough moment," an epiphany, and offers it as a gift to us as well as to the beloved. May we all have such revelations.

Eleanor Reeds
Hastings, Nebraska

Whom Have You Ever Loved From Choice Rather Than Habit

This life is not inevitable but a forest of paths to be explored,
Mud caking to heavier and heavier boots. Now I have so many
Wide open spaces, I keep longing for the canopy and charting
The only possible course. Nurturing the fig trees, I must also
Conserve water, spread fertilizer, prune dead branches to let
New life come forth and no storm bring them down to destruction.

I'm a grown woman still playing at miniature construction.
"Big house" says my son as his blocks reach up from the coffee table:
He giggles as Daddy drums on the pinkening skin of his belly.
My hands are burned and chipped and dry this October,
The clumsiness of motherhood as all "owies" are both mine and his.
My scar is fading but there is his navel, an eternal sign of parasitical genesis.

To be radical is to be rooted, to pull up a world by the roots,
To be willing to forego the shade and to disturb the ecosystem,
To retill the soil, to let it rest, to nurture new growth with the labor
Of delicacy. To be radical is to be rad as long as it is only
A performance, a role–and to be radicalized by such an attitude.
To be a mother desperate to have that child back in her body.

Eleanor Reeds
Hastings, Nebraska

The Sandblaster

The sandblasting job
lasted about a month,
a summer job where I
loaded my own
sandbags, 20 to 30
        60-pound bags
over my head
        into a hopper,
in 90-degree heat,
        then blasted the piss
out of a boxcar,
        my head
and shoulders covered
by a non-ventilated
        canvas hood,
climbing up scaffolding,
and *Shit,* the black
blasting sand ran out.
        All for $12 an hour.
        Not bad
in those days.

About a week in,
my foreman asked, "Want
some overtime?"
        No thanks, sir.

Two weeks
after I quit,
I was still
coughing up
black mucus,
digging black

sand out
of my ears,
  and eyes.

My work buddy, John,
told me they had upgraded
  to ventilated
  hoods now,
  and offered a break
every hour. "You
should come back."
I told him I had a lead
on a forklift job.
  He smiled
then laughed.

Michael Catherwood
Omaha, Nebraska

The Last Act

It's my turn to sit with him,
the cancer rat having chewed him to nothing.

The hospice nurse explains that the end is near;
he is not able to speak,
yet she encourages me to talk to him.

The best part of our sibling relationship
involved discussions about books,
both of us lovers of history.

He read books with war/military themes;
I preferred biographies.

On this morning where words seem so useless,
I stumble to find a beginning point to say something
to ease him toward the end.

I recall a biography of Harry Houdini,
so I chatter on about him—that he
assumed a stage name, that a number of people
believed he was a fraud, that he appeared in movies,
but his greatest fame came with escape acts.

That's all I can think of, so I switch topics
but just end up babbling about childhood memories.

The priest arrives; I leave the room to take a break—
say a prayer—have a cry.

Later when I return, Houdini has performed his magic
on my brother,
breaking off his chains of life.

Becky Faber
Lincoln, Nebraska

The Piano

When I saw my auntie, she had a cut on her cheek
and her finger fractured, fallowed to her ring.
She said a string snapped and the lid fell
while tuning the piano. Not that night her husband
chased her through the house with a knife
soused in his sherry suit. All winter she was missing,
came out marred and macerated with the spring.
Did she bury her diamond band under the
bridal bush, does she see herself hollow, puncture
through the pasture grass like a phantom?
Sometimes she hears the piano playing when she
walks inside from the garth and garlands
almond branches blooming by the bed. Her dead
children coming in like birds from the moors,
      wind beating the dark briars of their daddy.

Anastasia K. Gates
Palmyra, Pennsylvania

We are a dying breed,

those of us with names like Margie, Susan, Marcia, Doris,
Darlene, those of us who play it by ear, who cook without
recipes, not needing to look on-line to make devilled eggs,
strawberry jelly, stuffed peppers, drop noodles, apple pie.

And gathered around this buffet table we've all helped to lay,
our forks and paper napkins tucked beneath sturdy paper plates,
we dig in—but politely, carefully, masterfully—to sample what
fare, what tender morsels we've managed to bring to the table.

Yes, judgements are made—Brenda's quiche is a bit overbaked,
Mary is always a little heavy-handed with the garlic—but we've
all known thin days, tasteless times, so are grateful now
for the domestic bounty of these golden years.

Yes, rurban gals that we are, so different yet so similar in our
ways and means, we can't help—despite our breeding, our dabbling
in different fields, our remembrances of those who've wandered on
to greener pastures—but to gladly, guiltlessly feed. And the room

grows quiet, quieter than a meadow at mid-morning,
as we sit about, plates in hand, drinks at our heels, taking in
what each of us has contributed, savoring the knowledge
of years spent together—apart—together again.

For this half hour or so, sorrow is stilled, troubles forgotten,
hunger abated. And then somebody brings out a Ball jar of peaches
Denise had put by a couple years ago—before the mastectomy,
while she was still home. Soundlessly we pass the jar,

each of us dipping into the sweet, sweet brine, to pull up
a glistening moon, to plop it on our smeared plate and fork it,
bit by bit, into our open mouth, taking in kitchen, orchard,
field, deft hand, sure eye, warm sun, wide open sky.

Jan Mordenski
Farmington Hills, Michigan

Siltcoos River Canticle

The heron wades, stalking what—
minnows, tadpoles?—among waterweeds,
in the overhang of moss-wrapped spruce
along the slow and silent Siltcoos
speckled with the ripples of water-
skippers and droplets from our paddles
as we drift like maple leaves
in our kayaks, quiet, even
the dog, who in the bow
strains at her leash, wanting
to run across the smooth green
floor to Robin's boat, two dragon-
flies mating above before they zip off
in an azure flash like tiny lightning
soundless as we are, quiet enough
to hear mallard ducklings peep
in the shallows, snowy plovers
among the pale dunes which tower
above the river between walls
of old-growth—and then the roar
and rush of a log truck down 101,
just hidden among the firs,
and over the transept of a bridge
erupting from north to south bank
where suddenly we
are the water-skippers,
motes in a great cathedral,
drifting, leaving no trace.

Sean Bentley
Eugene, Oregon

Homeless Woman Drowns in Pond

Face down in the scum, hair the color
of brown seaweed, she was just there
by the new walking trail, one bright
fall morning.

The horror of Tulane student joggers
made them wish that Harvard
had accepted them to the safest campus
on God's New England earth.

All morning the police took down names;
the EMTs fished her out like any
dead reptile, the gator that charms
from a distance.

Theories were thick as autumn leaves,
though the most popular was an accident,
a "kerplunk" in the night heard only
by the owl or tree frog.

Not mad Ophelia or Dido scorned,
she was someone surely missed,
her wet clothes clinging like a shroud,
one eye open in pain.

William Miller
New Orleans, Louisiana

Grass Soup

In flight we had no time
To honor our dead.
Tipis fell burning beside
Smoldering cooking fires.
Food and blankets trampled underfoot.
Many barefoot in the snow.
      Joseph thought to save our meager band
By herding us into the mountains of the north.
Small boys, barely old enough to wear the pierced nose,
Wrangled the scant herd of spotted-rump ponies.
Everyone carried bundles of salvaged goods.
Even the dogs were saddled with rawhide packs.

Biting cold stalked our path like hungry wolves.
The deepening northern snows held no game.
      Finally, we slaughtered one of the ponies
For food that did not fill all the aching bellies.
We pulled half-digested grass
From the steaming gut to make grass soup
For the babies with swollen bellies.
We would have boiled our moccasins
But there were so few.

Jerry F. Prater
Donnellson, Illinois

Emily as a Blue Canary

Spiritual ruin only comes
when you stop listening
to Emily's strange bird
impression. She's convinced
three dozen spam callers
she's stuck in a small cage
inches from a cracker.
I don't think canaries want
crackers, but I want
every home warranty
company that calls us
to believe that they do.
I want Emily's broken song
& occasional human word
recorded so the next time
one of our rockets is sent
to space they have something
to delight the closest aliens.
I'm delighted every time
she's playful for no reason
other than my attention.

Darren Demaree
Columbus, Ohio

Sophia

Five fingers from two hands inside
my mouth prodding, poking, cutting,
stay still, don't move your tongue, the dental
surgeon snaps under the angry-yellow light
muted by sunglasses, are they sunglasses?

He removes his steel instrument and sighs,
then tries again, his instrument clattering against
teeth. *It's her tongue,* he murmurs to his assistant.
Sorry, I slur, squirming in the slick black seat
straining to keep my too small mouth with its
bothersome tongue-tied tongue open.

I cringe and push push push it all down,
the dentist does not realize I am suffocating …
I go to my happy place where Sophia the eagle resides
in a tree by the hidden lake under the warm yellow globe
where my silent screaming ebbs.

Sophia understands pain. I don't know how I know,
I just know. We commune without talking, Sophia and me …
it's quiet by the lake, the loons have gone to where loons go.

Move your head to the right, his voice knifes my thoughts
and I remember the tall thin white man, who loomed over the
brown seven-year-old girl, his black shadow jagged and sharp
I want to beat your face in, and I had stood cold on the
sizzling pavement and said nothing.

The drill now, deeper and deeper, my fingers dig into the
armrests, I gag stillness as my adoptive father's fingers
roam, his tongue licks my neck, breath suspended, suffocating, I push it
down down down, the scalpel presses like the knife against

my chest, my ex in a rage—he just might kill me
this time. If I say nothing, I might live …

in the dental chair I breathe in and out, in and out, in and out, there's
    Sophia again, lifting me,
holding me. she could go anywhere, be anywhere, be anything but she
    sits on top of the
undulating spruce tree feathers fluffed and ruffled, pinhole-eyes wide

I am on a bed or a chair, the creak of a door,
wait it's the floor; the dentist shifts his weight.
Almost done, he says. I remove the glasses
to see the bloody instruments and
gauze on the tray. I think about still tongues.

Sophia lets the wind take her, empyreal
black on white, white on black, talons ready,
we rise. Our screams echo wide.

Charmaine Arjoonlal
Yukon, Canada

Early Onset

In the spring, twelve cardinals against the window.
Light that dappled on the glass like marmalade;
three with eyes that wouldn't shut.
At thirteen, my sister and I took turns
upstairs in bed, dark, with headphones
set to white noise, some online challenge
intended to instill fear.
I waited, prone, for some creature
that never came.
When we removed the birds,
their heads dropped like buds,
fog green as dusk around each body.
There was never any explanation,
or one that would quite suffice.
What was meant to cause distress
only gave way to understanding.
Sometimes, for years after,
in the dark a rush of wings
would come from nowhere in particular.
A sudden pause, a person listening,
my life looming like a man's life
above me, but nothing outside the window.
We were girls, then; we couldn't expect
anything to save us.

Meggie Royer
Minneapolis, Minnesota

The Mirror

She left
a mirror compact
with fingerprints
from a year
I never speak aloud.

The kind
that catches light
just enough
to show
what memory won't.

I keep it
in a drawer
with loose change
and small
forgotten things.

Not even
my reflection
stays
long.

Gordan Struić
Zagreb, Croatia

Lepidopterist

Linda lived with Wendy in the oldest
house in the county about a mile
out of town. Its attic
was perfect, with its peaked ceiling
rafters, for where Linda
needed to place cocoons: warmth
always at a slant, giant incubator
full of dust mites and pollen.

Lepidopterist, Linda's passion was
emerging wings and she and Wendy
rented the place for their nursery.
Wendy helped tuck the finger-tip-sized
swaddles into the crooks of beams
smelling of old forests and honey.

Wendy's calling was horticulture
and she hoed a full acre for root settings,
food for every pattern
of fragile transformation.

I remember thinking, back then,
about collaborative love. Wondering
how many swallowtails and luna moths
slept inside of me and who would
find the house where we could raise them?

Who would plant fields of hungry
beauty? And how many
would even survive into spring
when Linda and Wendy walked hand-

in-hand up the rickety steps
to witness a steeple of wings?

Joanne Clarkson
Port Townsend, Washington

December

Nineteen degrees and I'm standing in the sun that streams
in through the front window. I'm eating a sweet
Fuji apple watching a fight between two gray squirrels.
One seems much thinner, unhealthy, and is soon chased away.
I've been thinking about the homeless in Minneapolis,
how they make it through the winter.
It's much easier in Key West or Miami.
I've heard there's a large homeless population in Honolulu.
I don't like the cold. Never have. Maybe because
I was born in Sault Ste. Marie, Michigan,
and caught pneumonia three times before the age of ten.
But this isn't about me. I'm alive and warm
in my three bedroom two bath bungalow.
It's about the thin sick squirrel that lost the fight
and where he ran away to. I can't think of the word.
It's right on the tip of my tongue.
Something to do with different forms of failure
maybe? Variations of failure?
I've never been to Minneapolis in the winter.
But I know they have sick squirrels there
and homeless, of course. Where do they run off to?
As I stand here in the warm window
watching sun streaming in on the victor.

Andy Roberts
Columbus, Ohio

She/Her (13 Years at the Shelter)

I noted today
my growing mental file
of women, no more than
two degrees of separation
and a baby
all dead
by men, possessive and possessed.
Organized chronologically
first to latest, but not last.
Because she won't be the last.

Details bob to the surface
periodically, the way
the river gives up her secrets
in the spring.
I remember
lacerated liver.
Little red flags quivering
on the side of the road.
Her mother's haunted eyes.

And how they always know
it's coming

Mandy VanLaningham
Beatrice, Nebraska

Boulevard des Capucines, 1873–1874

After the painting by Claude Monet

The carioles, half-hidden by trees, took
　　　on Parisian passengers
or left them off amid the frenzy
　　　of humanity on its way
to the Salon, perhaps a concert

　　　where they might
hear something by Rameau or Berlioz,
　　　or to a bookstore where Flaubert,
Hugo, or Balzac lived
　　　in gilded silken pages.

They took in, as well,
　　　the *odeurs de civilisation*—
horse manure and the best perfume,
　　　cigar smoke from
the Canary Islands, the finest
　　　pipe tobacco,
and, of course, body odor,
　　　ripe even in winter.

The sounds of the city
　　　symphonized their ears—
hoof and foot crunch
　　　in urban slush,
horse whinnies, leather creakings,
　　　coughs and sneezes beside
the grey bustle of commerce.

They strolled and rode within
　　　le movement de la vie—
naïve, innocent, ignorant

of what awaited their
children and grandchildren—
     trench death, mustard gas,
lice and foot rot, bayonets
     and bombs. The peace,
the pace, of the Boulevard des Capucines
     preoccupied them, distracted
them from the onrushing
     barbarism creeping down
les rues de l'histoire.

Charlie Brice
Pittsburgh, Pennsylvania

Nostalgia

I still see you sometimes.
I'm walking and you're
on a bus, or you're at a bus stop
when I'm driving past. blonde
in my mirror there, just
for a moment. like in the bathroom
in my london bedsit in 2011
or thereabouts, brushing
your teeth. look: I am married, and you're
still in london. it's a two hour flight.
college was a long
time ago. I'm a dog
watching the door.
can you stop showing up
for a moment
every now and then
please?

DS Maolalai
Dublin, Ireland

A Many, and a One

One afternoon, the forest
of pre-spring bare branches around the house
teemed with black foliage.

As soon as that whole shady throng erupted,

the sky went dark. If a plurality
of crows is a "murder," here was a "massacre,"

yet we saw a community with common cause.

By morning, branches were empty,
skies clear of heavy traffic, though a cardinal
of another avian college kept watch

from the alabaster transept of a nearby birch:
a candle we did not light—

but neither had we cursed the darkness.

Russell Rowland
Meredith, New Hampshire

Joy

It was a photo that you
wanted to like: one of the
last ones, yet you would have liked
a sharper image, not this
awkward airborne pose. The way
pictures changed things. The way things
changed on you, boys growing up,
for instance, to be men when
you liked them as they were. You
say, this is California;

you remember the day, and
your husband says, no, don't you
see; it's Boston, near the old
house. The park where they played. But
you're crying; you say, who took
this shot; you can barely see
the kid for the blurring, and
he says, no, don't you see; he
was running. And you see it:
he's headed somewhere; he's on

his way; his feet are off the
ground. You say, I remember
that day; he was running and
holding something. You say, it's
blurred; you say you don't like that
picture. No, he's not holding
anything, your husband says.
Look again; there's nothing there.
He's holding nothing; don't you
see; he can't hold it: the joy.

Becky Kennedy
Jamaica Plain, Massachusetts

All of Us Eventually

There's always a diagnosis now,
cholesterol, glaucoma, unruly genes
ticking. But we're not talking about me,
we're talking about your father—
how all he will eat these days is
graham crackers and milk.
The morphine, the prowlers
he imagines creeping along the wall.
Or maybe we're talking about all of us
eventually, how everything ends in ashes.
We blended my sister's with her son's,
gray mist in the celebrants' lungs
or you on a chartered boat,
your grandmother's urn—
fishing nets discreetly stowed,
waiting to unfurl, to drag the water
like fingers of memory searching
for a slippery word. Maybe
it will go that way for me, lid unscrewed,
my ashes tipped overboard, a bloom
of jellyfish surfacing. First, they're sequins
rising through dream, then the edges of ideas
pulsate dark to light, every beautiful thing
I've forgotten, rising.

Melody Wilson
Beaverton, Oregon

Wild Swimming

Whether Virginia and Vita
ever swam naked together in
Kenwood Ladies' Bathing Pond,
I cannot know. But I imagine
them skinny dipping in that
teardrop-shaped pool on
Hampstead Heath—Vita
sinuous and lithe as swans
who glide the green-blue
surface, spindly Virginia
a retiring, long-legged
heron wading, waiting
nearer shore.

She, whose fictional child
aspired to waves and
lighthouse, one day
weighted her pockets with
rocks, prudently set down
hat and cane on the bank
of River Ouse, stepped out
from the shallows, released
her body to water, her words
to eternity.

Linda M. Lewis
Lindsborg, Kansas

Beach Day

There's an ocean in me.
I don't know when it happened,
but the waters rise
until salt burns my throat
and I can't breathe.
I pull the jagged coral from my teeth,
and cut myself open
from collarbone to sternum
and when the dam of my ribs breaks
I dump seawater and bile all over our bed.
It's endless.
Wet sand and colorful fish,
rotted wood and plastic trash.
It spills and spills
until our home is flooded
With a mess I can never clean.
In the aftermath
as I gasp and cough and sob
you tell me
how thoughtful it was
for me
to bring the beach to you.

D.S.L. Sherlock
Philadelphia, Pennsylvania

The Potted Flower

We were meant to bloom
in vast open spaces—
where water, land, and birds made their homes,
where sunlight spilled over the wide waters,
where the red chalice of the sun
merged with the reflection
of our blossoming, ripened bodies,
where the eastern winds
trembled through us again and again,
where the valleys are in full bloom.

Yet I have bloomed—
in your flowerpot,
with all the constraints of the world.
A thirsting being,
sipping water drop by drop,
without the rushing streams,
without the whispering winds,
caught in the cramped struggles
of your small corner—
I bloom,
on the tiny mound of my dreams
within this pot.

Sushil Kumar
Dumka, India

Anhedonia, April

Suburban vinyl siding—mildewed, stained,
in bleak near-spring when hopelessness prevails—
sparks dreams of childhood summers, coastal Maine,
silver-gray shingled cottages and sails
on the horizon. He decides to pry
his dismal clapboards off and start again
with virgin cedar shakes, a hopeful try
at how things used to be. Time to begin.

He nails the first few overlapping rows
before despair sets in. Woodpeckers pound
into exposed tarpaper. In the holes
finches build ragged nests. The project founders
into paralysis. He grows morose—
his woe too deep to nail on just that house.

Elizabeth Stoessl
Portland, Oregon

The Man on the Stoop

The man on the stoop has sat stoic,
steely-eyed and silent for what feels
like three decades. Always sucking
on a Marlboro Red, craggy fingers
weaving through bits of a beard
once auburn, now gray and fraying.
Pointy knees sticking out of nylon
basketball shorts, even when ice
glazes trees and skin starts to
prickle. A faithful, ink-black lab who
ignored squirrels snored at his feet
for many years, then a growling
spotted mutt with yellowed teeth.
Then just cans of Bud or Miller Lite.

He has heard the close-up crunch
of nasty fender-benders, watched
the wheels of careless parkers spin
away with Pete's Towing. He has
been doused with drops of sweat
from sticky runners, nearly toppled
by the whoosh of zooming scooters.
He has seen hulky garbage crews
lift, toss and beep, wordless bus
stop patrons pace, board and stare.

He has felt envious at the angst of
boy-girl sidewalk spats, marveled
at lovers strolling under the moon.
He has wondered where it all went,
when his inside tap seemed to run
dry. When he became invisible,

a sad, outdoor fly-on-the wall on
the corner of Rhodes and 19th.

Susan Miller
Arlington, Virginia

Adolescent Atheist

The wrath of God is the tantrum of an abandoned child.

An only girl in a family of boys
their big sister became a mirage in lost time

Before the youngest knew what time was
until the oldest knew what death does

After the crash, after the phone calls
until the relatives arrived from afar

After the hospital, after endless vigils until
the doctors gave us all permission to give up hope

The youngest looked askance at an empty sky
said, *deities too are all destined to die*

Now he visits her crypt in the mausoleum
like an acolyte in a wax museum

Like an anchorite in a house of doubt
cursing god and rehearsing hurt

Reviving her blonde beauty and her
brief life cut short by some dumb drunk

Out for a Sunday binge post-prayers
running red lights to road-test blind faith

The crash was a T-bone, a film cliche
she went through the windshield while they

Survived to kill another day, another
young mother brought to roadside slaughter

It was back in '64 when his sister was killed
he screams at all gods and bad drivers still.

Richard Collins
Sewanee, Tennessee

To Captain Hazelwood, on Alexander Mountain

High winds scrubbing Exxon from the feathers
    of the noon sun—like a child who's thumbed
the soap-scummed pinions of an eider chick
    choking on Prince William Sound, sea-squelched,
splayed in the blue of a television
    in nineteen ninety, set weird with static,
bleared between such stints of trial footage
    as sterilize the light that's coalesced
around this first of all the memories
    I have—there's (forty years thence) fire spreading,
shiny as an oilslick, down-mountain, poised
    to lick some gaudy mansion in the hills.
And why not let it feast for all I've learned
    by any broadcast since? That the seabirds
drowned, iridescent. Hundreds of thousands.
    That pinesmoke hooks its fingers in the lung.
That nature spends, Father, and what is spent
    stays spent. Still, just past their long disguises
of hanging ash, my mountains reappear—
    lovely as ducklings, feathered with black trees.

Nathan Manley
Windsor, Colorado

Trees

Cloistered, trees dead
and dying and stripped
for winter, wrap my sky
in crooks of skeletal
fingers, limbs thick
and cracked, some thin
enough twist around
my arm, remind me
that once I climbed
trunks just to look
down on my friends
and then to look out
at horizons yet to cross,
and now become walls
broken by gray sky,
that hold my spirit
here a moment longer
before I drift away
with fall's last dead leaves.

Richard Dinges
Walton, Nebraska

Fall

Overnight it's grown too cool
to keep windows open.
I awake chilled
to vacant sky, the sun
out of sight.

I'm unprepared.
I need to wear something warm,
but it's all packed away.
I find long sleeves, tall socks,
stick my sandals in the closet.

Already this descent
into winter, already wind alone
at play on the beaches
where waves spike,
sand hard as tundra.

In the yard, the geraniums
are sparse, with leaves that curl
at the edge. Dried blossoms
I haven't removed
stand shriveled and dark.

Eleven years since fall
and death came swiftly on,
my father in his tomb,
sky pressing clouds
upon the stones.

Is this how Persephone felt?
Still flushed with summer's warm
forgetting, called back to the underworld,
creeping down a black cavern,
every moment a farewell?

Kate Deimling
Brooklyn, New York

Triple Haiku for the Crows Who Bathe in the Thunderstorm on Beach Boulevard

little black birds sit,
pray along the powerline,
heads held to the sky–

washed, but not quite clean.
their song drowned out by engine
roar, this world never

their own. for this sweet
moment, though, they are happy:
baptized in clouds' cries.

Jillian Atwood
Fleming Island, Florida

Night Weeding

In an effort to get myself out more in public
I joined my building's community garden,
and they assigned me weed duty to test my mettle.
But my sleep cycle has shifted again, I just can't help it,
and now I'm fast asleep from dawn till dusk,
so I weed at midnight, when no one is around.
It's hard work, and I'm as green as the garden is,
learning how to fletch my arrows as I go.
I weed silently by flashlight amid hoots and rustles,
a guidebook open in the chilly grass beside me
delineating which species I should pull from the long beds.
I grab trifoliate leaves and tug and tear,
plucking the hearty thistled vines from the stalks
of tomatoes, peas and beans, bell peppers.
Every day in the waning sun the pernicious plants grow back,
and every night I pull them up again,
tearing succulent white roots from the soil they carry on with.
Come on, I tell us both through gritted teeth,
Fraternizing is overrated.
Like a witch, I work from midnight till three,
pulling my coat closer and plucking and pulling.
In my zeal I tear out a few flowers sometimes,
but I'm still learning the trade, and I've no complaints yet.
Two hours before sun-up, I dust my hands off, return inside
and mouse off to bed with dirt under my fingernails.
Lord, what a difficult life this is, sometimes.

Sean Eaton
New England

Nesting Dolls

The air tonight is a nesting
doll. The call of cicadas
around the sound of bird
settling into nest around
the rustling of something
beyond the yard in the
leaves around the smell
of jasmine around the
giving away of consciousness
that surrounds
what might be the last
of the day's worries or
the start of the night's
fears. How often is it,
after a pandemic and
during climate rages,
to have a seed of fear
stuck into our teeth, a pea
beneath our mattress.
So perhaps the jasmine
masks decomposition
that will bloom in tomorrow's
sun. Perhaps the distant stirring
is a coyote that will take
the neighbor's cat in its jaw
and shake. Perhaps even
the night air carries virus.
What's calming in the world
has always been a mask. Ask
the remains of a small child
found in a cave in Siberia with
tooth marks in bone. Ask
the child's mother, long dissolved

into breath distributed across
the globe and water long traveled
to the ocean. Ask that nesting bird
so weary it doesn't hear
the neighbor's cat. Who
are we rooting for on this earth?

Danielle Hanson
Irvine, California

Garage

There is a fascination with what scares us most. The fire,
the garage, watching it burn across the street. The house
had been empty since the Smiths moved out. We knew
the fire could not harm anyone. A mystery as to how it started,
the homeless perhaps—except we'd seen none around here,
not in this neighborhood. I'm scared to death of fire,
and yet I sat in the rocking chair on my own front porch,
watching it burn. Watched it burn down to studs
that glowed orange, down to the foundation, the flames
licking around the edges of random piles of things
left in it. I watched it cast orange glow until
I finally remembered my cell on the table next to me
and called the fire squad to tell them it was burning.
It was so far along, they came and simply watched too.

Andrea Dickens
Mesa, Arizona

Ars Poetica

Novices think writing is like strolling into a Monte Carlo casino
filled with sparkly evening gowns and James Bond tuxedos
and stepping up to the roulette table to place a bet.
If the ball doesn't bounce into the right slot by the third try,
one should have the *savoir faire* to walk away with a smile,
head high, back straight as a martini stirrer.

But we know it's like an old farm wife visiting her son in prison
every week, gaining the goodwill of the guards
with cinnamon-scented coffee cakes, banana bread,
maybe some rum balls in the run-up to Christmas.
On her son's birthday, she brings a luscious chocolate cake
into which she's baked a small hacksaw, confident
he'll ply it only at 3 a.m. (while everyone else snores),
patiently slicing away at each bar over his solitary window
for as long as it takes to set himself free.

Patricia L. Hamilton
Jackson, Tennessee

When the Swans Remembered the Stars

The swans have begun to dream again.
Not of lakes or reeds or grain,
but of black suns
and bone-colored moons
pulling at the tendons of their wings.

Each winter, they forget.
They return to the frozen rivers,
eyes clouded with static,
feet blood-warm and blistered.
They nest in graveyards now,
in the ribs of machines
long buried beneath the snow.

But some nights,
under a sky too still,
they lift their heads
and scream.

No one knows why the swans scream.

The old lore says
they came from elsewhere—
not evolved, but exiled.
Banished from a war of light
where wings were weapons,
and memory, a curse.

Their songs once mapped the cosmos.
Each note a coordinate.
Each cry a warning.

Now   they   sing   in   fragments,
like   a   radio   tuned   wrong,
and   children   wake   with   nosebleeds
and   visions   of   burning   skies.
Some   draw   strange   constellations
on   the   walls   in   charcoal,
stars   that   do   not   belong
to any sky we've named.

Last   migration,
a   swan   flew   straight   into   the   sun.
No   deviation.
No   cry.
Just ash.

And   somewhere   beneath   the   ice,
in   the   drowned   chambers
of   a   forgotten   observatory,
the red light blinks again.

The   swans   have   begun   to   dream.
This   time,
they will not forget.

Gloria Ogo
Norfolk, Virginia

Haven

For Max

The wind blows the oak's branches back like

A head of riotous hair, and despite the big
Bluster he is sleeping peaceful at his center

Feeling like forever. He knows how little of his life
The drift covers. He knows that when he dies
Skin will be the last thing on his mind.

Not that he isn't glad to have this half of him that
Is weightless—it's just he hasn't been taught like the
Rest of us how to pick up the ground and get going.

There is this tin container where my heart is,
And that instant whisper of a *yes*: enough
To have me wrangling the contents jostled out.

Would you stuff the bindle for just a whiff?
Would you be blinded by that smell of blood
In the water? Tell me you would. Tell me the next

Time a storm comes stirring up the hearth, we'll
Be ready. We'll hunch close to the damp Earth and
Hold on tight to everything that keeps us still,

　　　　　　　Makes us untouchable.

Jake Wallace
Little Rock, Arkansas

Levi

This morning,
I watched the mix of warm water and milk
bubble through cinnamon, cloves, cardamom,
and a pinch of salt like fractures in the lithosphere.

In a few hours,
my daughter will fissure like earth's crust
birthing a mountain, from her body's warm river
a slippery boy soft as a moth, all head and belly,
will arrive to a sky of , before landing
against my daughter's milky breasts—his own bubble.

His scent like cake next to the salty skin of his parents,
their eyes will pool oases, and bodies will hew a cocoon
against the too fast future of wings and flight. Not today.
Today, he'll swaddle in fog of faces, fuzzy voices of *strangers*.

Susan Mason Scott
Madison, Indiana

World News & Commentary

The News is too much with us; breaking fast,
purveyance of algorithmic infoporn
fed by coal calories and every last
<media> blob a spoonful of sugar
to help the consumption go down, a
wholesale retell of a creed outworn.
   The News is a world of thumbs prancing
limply around screens to be lifted, reborn
when cued to tap *here* for deliverance
from the couch to the chyrons that con-
nect and monetize the moves, a tap-dance
in tune with the times and tribal fifes.
   Yet News is how I knew to decipher
the weight of microplastics in my brain.

The News is a bane filtration quagmire
with no solution to the mutagens
but renunciation and funeration—
entombment of this toxic sordid boon
where every shareholder is now defiled:
air, water, land, food, us, them, the truth.
   The News is that even Gods are mutating—
witness Triton's tail! or verge of Proteus
or Aletheia's alternative facts. Jesus.
With great power came great absurdities.
And adding brain cancer to his burnout,
it's harder to imagine happy Sisyphus.
   Yet News is where I find the cross-
word puzzles to free me from that abyss.

The News is when my grip grips my face,
draining transient tears from my eyes:
Extra—Extra—You've already vanished—so
Awaken! (sorry, but you keep falling asleep)—
and time is not money, not monetary—
who planted that blighted metaphor?
   The News is that attention is loving.
Metaphor healed. Now, Goodness, let me go
outside and commune with the daffodils,
commiserate as we all haste away,
coauthor poems, maybe canticles,
of earth and sun and limits lest we die.
   The News down here is that every day
is a slow day for news:

        Love your home, *Terrestrial.*
        The rest is commentary.

David Alm
Mount Pleasant, Michigan

* Alludes to a few poems and borrows obviously from Wordsworth's "The
World Is Too Much With Us," from which it takes part of the first line
and a number of other phrases.

Disappointment

wilting, if there must be one stem,
greenhouse cultivated,
one root of truth,
will the universe be lonely without us? Sappy, will it yearn
for we great apes
like a flower desires petals, colors ablaze
with new life?
Withering hope is soon plucked
from people's pots,
no more symbolic buds, sly fragrance, or green thorns.
Astonishing, these stamens
and pistils! Doom
now pollinates our apologies. Soon, no more
crimson roses to say
"Forgive me"
to paramours wronged. The fated,
hellacious sun
is a dying blossom, too.
You and me,
jilted from all memories, unromantically forgotten
by wild loves—
foxglove, oleander, hemlock,
mountain laurel,
and all our poison enemies gone—all
oblivion. My one word,
like a dandelion against my lips to sum up the human bloom,
is not "love,"
for "disappointment" echoes,
then it doesn't.

Dana Stamps, II
Riverside, California

Carpe Kairos

I count falling leaves before they touch the ground;
but Autumn isn't cool enough for running children.

Time is a green forest wall; trees beside a dusty,
back road littered with cans, bottles and paper
tossed through windows when no one is looking.

I've broken paper promises before:

forgetting to count party favors
when I know the wind blows glitter to the floor;
whatever I hold inside.

If leaves didn't fall, I would color plain skies gray.
If leaves did not fall, autumn would bypass winter
when I purchase time on credit:

promises that cup blue skies and fallen leaves
in both hands. If leaves were falling I would know.

PM Flynn
Edenton, North Carolina

Bigfoot

It was a simple hoax.
I drove to the woods
put on a hairy costume
then ran along the forest's edge.

People in the distant carpark
clamoured with their phones
and within seconds I'd become
a blurred image of bigfoot

reposted for days.
When the interest faded
I weaved between the pines
but this time bullets rang

the stones at my feet
so I ran into dusty darkness
until I reached a clearing.
As I parted dripping ferns

a hairy creature looked up
from drinking at a pool
and bared its teeth
then started to run.

The next day
I was outed as a fake
and humiliated
and I was glad of it.

I posted images
of my hairy body suit
until the hunters went home.
Now I follow footprints

between dripping pines
to the muddy lake
where every shadow
draws breath.

Paul Bavister
Shaftesbury, England, UK

Mid-April

Walking this sorry neighborhood
I feel houses shudder as I pass.
No one's home or everyone's home,

faces impressed on the windows
long after their owners have died.
No wonder dogs bark desperately.

No wonder limbs snap off maples
and destroy their perfect symmetry.
Much of the landscape is marsh,

secret marsh that troubles one's sleep.
Spring peepers peep so loudly
they inhibit conversation with

the women pushing strollers
or walking fluffy Samoyeds
or noodling along like me without

planning the rest of their lives.
The houses regret so much.
Their legends don't apply to me

so I'd rather not hear how grandma
died of boredom, how the youngest
sibling went crazy on meth

and cooked and ate the family pets,
how Sis became a famous hooker.
The dogs bark, the surviving people

rake leaves with grim determination,
clearing for the fresh May flowers
with their misleading little smiles.

William Doreski
Peterborough, New Hampshire

In the Slow Spool of Summer

Once again: July.
The honey of June
still on my lips.

Air laden and ripe
with the sweetness
of summer.
Hot emerald leaves absorb
the sticky heat
of the sun
and breathe out a cloying
molasses.

I have never tasted a summer like this.

I have never been alive until now.

I float my body down the dappled stream and I'm 14 again,
convinced of my own immortality.

My summer overflows
with these days.
I cup them,
and sifting them through my hands,
they cascade
down from between my fingers
like golden coins
ringing against each other
as the pile grows:
a testimony to abundance.

Fig trees whose small green delights
are yet to weigh down their branches
hang in a heavy crescent over the water.

It is becoming August.

Summer is rounded
and I return to myself.
To the primordial pounding
in my chest
that sings in harmony
with the pace of all growing,
living things.

In sublime and languid euphoria
time spools out slowly
beneath the Jurassic palms.
Drunk on our midsummer mirth,
lifting naked from that river of youth,
we sun our bodies like lizards.

We have never known fear.
We will never taste death.

Donalyn White
Rialto, California

When Grandma Got Her Way

I saw grandpa slurp one last
roast beef puree
wash it down
with cold thick coffee
and a burp his eyes
wide to the white hall
lined with wheelchairs
little dried rivers
of mashed potatoes
flat on chapped lips
his jaw slack
his stare blank

he rolled back to bed
asked again
with his sweet rasp
who she was where
he parked the car
and she responded
right out front
as she unclamped the IV
in his purple wrist
twisted the morphine
dial released it all
and I watched the door

Ben Hyland
Sarasota, Florida

Fields

Cut hay makes ridges
like gopher burrows
after snowmelt

————

Gentle creeks fold uneven fields
like swooping caresses
from my father's old shirt

————

Cows, like unrisen dough,
munch frosted grass
in mid-August

Sam Huston
Leadville, Colorado

genius of interpretation

She's out of the past, wearing *Shalimar*.
Hippie goddess in a psychedelic gown
A cotton candy French twist
Black liner smile at her eyelid's edge
leukemia lipstick
Maybe her last standing ovation.
30 people in a masterclass
Spiked punch, little sandwiches of watercress and crab,
a seat on the Cleopatra couch
She slips off her bangles but not the rings.
She asks someone to take off her flats.
Her toes are knotted pink facsimiles

The host runs a reel to reel.
Early-sixties black-and-white.
She was the usual love interest,
wearing a white bikini, sexy/chaste
Small breasts
No one got fake boobs back then
If you were sexy, you were sexy.

Her voice crackles like AM out of range:

On location
Clouds of green-head flies on the beach
and men with bad breath,
The director barking orders from his
yacht.

The white bikini and the dark ocean
The stark glamorous shadows!
She was the best version she would ever be

She could have had less salad and more French food,

more red wine,
A husband instead of lovers
Even a child

Dry regret doesn't bring possibility
Like sex without coming night after night

On the yacht
After a night of making love
She once found an uncut diamond at the bottom of her Bloody Mary
This was not a proposal. She would not say yes.
Her lover said, *A diamond for every sunrise.*

Who had to die so she could scratch her name in a mirror?

Janet Belding
Mashpee, Massachusetts

Deliberations

I am your guide up the hillside
darkness around us while
somewhere above
the cat stretched out on a branch
wonders if we are worth
the trouble.

The path snakes between the trees
to the small dark building
set as far as
possible away from the cabin.

I stand outside and wait for you, my
back against the dark wood,
watching the water
on the lake shimmer, as it has
every day of my life
and of my youth

and in that moment I know how you are
seeing the cabin, the deep
woods, and my life.

Breathing the mountain air, I am the
scent of pine and cedar, of
scat and leaves in
the throes of transformation, and the
sound of bodies moving in
the branches overhead
is my oxygen.

Underneath our feet, the dark loam
is a deep familiar fragrance
like the scent of sex

in the cabin in the wide old bed with
noisy springs, where I again
guide you and

am filled with you, under the window
where starlight wanders
in between the
branches and dapples the white
sheets with a
forest painting

Judith Mikesch-McKenzie
Eugene, Oregon

The Blue Casket

I left it in the chapel,
the blue Century casket,
but depleted courage
kept my heart's racket
from reentering to verify
it hadn't rolled away
on the wooden bier—

a canoe to whisk it down
the carpeted hallways—
an impromptu last-ditch
escape—*Charon, take me
away.* I heard the wheels
turning—like gears in an old
clock—before it glided to a stop

in front of my desk in the lobby
—lid closed, a spray of orange
Gerbera daisies atop. And I'm pushing
it now, this casket atop this bier—

the thundering *clink, clink* of its
commute clacking like a freight
engine miles away, and the roar
grows louder as I push it faster

and faster back to the chapel,
back to the front of the room,
to rest between the sanctuary
floor candle stands—tall and red.

The pulsing echo fills the empty
room. I don't report its attempted
exit. Caskets can't move by
themselves. I know that.

Cat Dixon
Papillion, Nebraska

A Droplet Joyfully Leapt Out of the Wave

just for the joy of leaping
I let go of my mother's hand and jumped into the cold, dark lake

the crashing white noise of water disrupted the reflections
swans with wings poised open

who called the waters down from the glacier
I could not walk away from

so I walked backwards down the path
guiding my family past pond-flickering tadpoles

to the summer toboggans
no one wanted to slip-slide through the cerulean gentian with me

you have to keep your hands away from the rails
while your heartbeat leaps

and falls seaward
backwards off the boat into gold-laced water

I could barely breathe for elation
shoals, parties, orchestras of fish performing

an exalted symphony
underwater clicks and chirps, snaps and pops

burnt sienna cephalopods, silver-winged mālolo, iridescent mahimahi
readying themselves for the leap

Béthany Pozzi-Johnson
Maui, Hawaii

At Twelve

I planted new marigolds in eager earth
when the air smelled like spring. We rolled
in dewy grass, his curious nose nudging me.

In summer, we chased dandelion puffs and
escaped into the wind. He learned to paddle.
I learned to float.

During afternoons on the porch, the waning
sun blanketed shadows over us as we nestled
in for naps.

Our shared conversations between whimpers
and sighs moved smoothly from one day
into the next.

As snowflakes fell, he gripped my hand
harder than usual. Gentle teeth careful
not to hurt, leading me toward home.

When he was twelve, both our eyes, wet
and weary, could only focus on our
faces. We held on until we couldn't.

When I dream, sometimes he's a boy.
Sometimes he's a dog. His paw prints
from weeks ago are still pressed in the snow.

B.J. Burton
Berwyn, Pennsylvania

Sugar

My friends and I
got drunk
and
branded ourselves with lighters—
so we'd never forget that night.
What a shitty night
that was.

The asphalt
is
grey, like pastries.
At my childhood home,
I scratched my name into the driveway
and it's still there.

The bank seized the house
and now it's empty.
I crawled
in
through the broken window,
and found
that stuffed rabbit you thought was lost
in the move.

Cars will still run
with
sugar in the tank.
Not for long—but
as long as they need to.
On the side of some backroad,
a grey impala

bakes in the sun,
waiting.

Odin Meadows
Urbana, Illinois

Wondering

I knew a guy in high school who liked to hit dogs …
with his car. Well, I didn't really know him, but
my best friend once helped him clean blood

off his car's bumper after a foray on an otherwise
somnambulant suburban street. I wonder about him
every now and then: Is he doing 20-to-life for plowing

into a pro-abortion demonstration, killing three marchers
chanting "Our bodies. Our choice"? Or is he VP
of a hedge fund known for its acquisition of foundering

businesses, which he ruthlessly strips of workers before
selling off the remaining carcass of capitalism
gone amuck, pocketing millions in the process?

Or maybe he's just an average dad living in the 'burbs
with a picture-postcard yard, picture-postcard family,
and a tank-sized SUV for hauling trash to the dump

on Saturdays, who stays up late to cruise the internet
for crazy cheap deals, not-so-soft porn,
and videos of puppies being tortured.

Rick Blum
Bedford, Massachusetts

Sisters of the Bloody Sacred Heart

O Beautiful and specious nuns who three-edged
rulers across my fey fingers for learning sake,
who draped themselves in mourning rags,
and made their crotches sacred stock
and broke me from my deadly heritage,
who taught me dynasties of Angel kings
and Shakespeare in their mother tongue
so I might stand on corners anywhere
and catch the threads of metaphor
I might overhear. They gave their all—
what any bastard needs to pass.
       (that strangest love which is unkindest love)
Such patriots to the latinate
loved me more than church or state—
un-SKIed my compatriots
with bantam Anglo names
and did it all so they might pass
(Unkindness is the truest love).
       I pass.

John Horvath
Jackson, Mississippi

Reliquary in Hastings, NE

The freedom to run on polished steel,
whistles laughing in exhilaration,
while boxcars grumble at their heavy freight.
They rumble past white mountain elevators.

At the end of freedom, engines clothed
in sprawling graffiti, reds, oranges, greens, and blues,
swirling, and bubbling like lava lamps,
left to rot along missing rails and stops.

Barbara A. Meier
Lincoln, Kansas

As the Darkness Descends

In winter the night always arrives too soon—
a guest who appears at your door
before the wine is opened,
the table set, the roast in the oven.

Nonetheless you welcome him.
What else can you do?
After all, you two go way back.
You've been friends
as long as you can remember.

Well, one day not long from now
you'll be ready when the light
from the afternoon sun
flattens and pales
before it shines directly into your eyes
and begins to sink like a ship
struck by an iceberg,
slowly at first,
then seemingly all at once!

Still, the light remains—
a stubborn afterglow, colorful and beautiful
in its weakness.

You'll be ready to embrace the night,
grateful for the fading light
as the darkness descends.

Ed Meek
Somerville, Massachusetts

Santa's Down Time

December 15, every year without fail, Edith and Jim Walker
pump up their 10-foot tall, front yard inflatable Santa,
bushily bewhiskered, a study in red and white, except
for green mittens and black boots. His ensemble,
naturally, is topped with a floppy stocking cap.

He waves to one and all convincingly (for a lifeless
overgrown balloon). His reindeer sidekick, the red nose
a dead giveaway for you know who, prances in place.
They are tied down by sturdy twine and stakes.
Thus, they pose, one holiday season after another.

But this year, the sun rising on December 20, found
the twosome ripplingly flattened into overlapping shells.
Who knocked the wind out of them wasn't a mystery
for long. A security camera captured Micky and Carl
Simmons, two young brothers from down the street,

hilariously puncturing the none too impermeable balloons
with thin wooden skewers, video time-stamped 2:03 AM.
They knew the boys and their parents but casually.
Santa and Rudolph were provisionally allowed to repose
where they fell. On the 22nd, the Walkers hailed

the brothers who were bicycling in the neighborhood.
A brief and cordial interrogation and evidentiary viewing
resulted in shame-faced admissions and apologies
and earnest vows never to repeat such a nasty trick,
on anyone. They shook hands with the scofflaws,

assuring them their parents would remain none the wiser,
and the matter was closed pending the agreed upon
remedy. Come December 23, Santa and Rudolph, suitably

puffed up, stood tall and bouncy once more, chest wounds
duct-taped, antlers bobbing and ho ho ho-ing into January.

Philip Wexler
Bethesda, Maryland

She Goes Unacquainted with Gracefulness

In the predawn cold
a young woman sits on her front steps,
smokes a *toothbrush Marlboro,*
smells the jasmine growing next to her
that she'll bring in later,
and listens to the crashing bay
just a mile and a half away

Warm coffee and the sun on her face
—is there any other reason
to walk the mile and a half,
the morning birds chirping,
junkmen driving block to clock,
it doesn't matter which season.

The Sumo Oranges on the neighbor's tree
or the trees bare in winter,
the bay still chants. It calls to her
no matter the coastal weather,
the clock moves so slow
it hurts to watch it.

Tobi Alfier
Torrance, California

For Tomaž IV

In my tribe, decisions must be unanimous.
We do not wash our feet in the river,
we do not expose our skin to the sun,
never leave the shadows. We run across
the plains like recently released horses,
stir up the dirt and send spells of stones
shooting across the cosmos. Unscrupulous
amateurs to the exhibition frequently
lose consciousness, rebound only to fall
victim to promises no one could keep,
at least not considering the current landscape.
In my tribe, the resuscitation of magic
might lead to more enviable outcomes,
and boundaries disappear when we see beneath
our shrouds the loud thump of the heart
sounds the same no matter your position.
In my tribe, we never wonder about the creator,
we have no story about how we came to be here.
We take down the names who leave no observation,
who contribute nothing and merely complain
about the lack of anything but the sky,
who ask how we expect to last with no light.
We perform last rites for those who take flight,
never return from the sky and we don't wonder why.

Devin Gmyrek
Eliot, Maine

On Deck

I saw a cooper hawk in the yard
The day John Ashberry died.
It spent the day circling. Only landing
Once: small candy bar wrappers
Caught in an updraft. Still, I listened
And waited for the call and response
Of the crows.

The poems don't come. The rhythm
stays chopped: her hair dyed
Gray—it's in vogue—it's in style.
I stand beneath her jagged mist
as we listen to the call and response
Of the crows.

The turkeys in the backyard call out
"the bubbles will fix your troubles"
before they charge a squirrel
to roast on the fire they've made
out of broken limbs and dried leaves.
They eat listening to the call and response
Of the crows.

The chickadees and rabbits, rabbits
And sparrows ignore it all:
These men care nothing of poetry
only protection. They stock guns and bullets
(so many shiny pieces of metal!)
In basements and shelters waiting
For a sign to cut through the response
of the crows.

The crows back then were fat,
so very, very fat. They sat

On branches around town and told us
All the news we wanted to hear.

John Rodzvilla
South Hamilton, Massachusetts

The Day I Met You

I learned to read your face that winter,
when I sat at the Costa sipping away my life;
it was a harmless cup of black coffee,
brewed and stirred in the dim-lit room
where customers stormed like a train station.
You marooned my eyes on the pavement.
From here, I saw you gliding like a paper,
for whom the wind was such a racket
that I stuffed my ears with earplugs
not knowing you hid within the wind's whiff,
your feet never haggling for retention,
your eyes shut like a wintry night.
A halo of patience lumbered on your lips;
I knew then that I found my lost item.
I came to you with the moon in my eyes
and a yellow sky banging on my head,
that this afternoon was not for a lonely tea.
Convinced that you would turn in my way,
and cast away this heavy body within you,
I curated my face into a naked god,
my heart prostrated for the things I desired.
I left my coffee cold, my mouth slit,
my spoon spinning out the tears from my eyes,
as my traffic turned from red to amber and green.
This thing I have for you must be a spirit
else how could I have given up my pot of time,
more precious than a thousand pots of coffee,
to stand before you a moron, simpleton, derelict,
the reality of undead dreams,
hoping that your smile would stitch me,
and scrub this sanctuary I transgressed,
knowing that neither of us shall die of things
that we desire before we devour them.

I wrote your name and number on my teeth,
went home dizzy like a stumbling foot,
that a queen like you kissed a lark like me,
stealing my remains away.

Jonathan Chibuike Ukah
London, England, UK

Marlboros

They whisper awful lies

You are nothing
The quicker you are gone,
the better it'll be, they say

I do not deserve to die this way

Unless
Perhaps I do
Maybe I am wrong
I don't want to believe it,
But they insist that it's true

They offer to hold my hand,
To walk this path with me
They cannot desert me
With me, they'll always stand

Their whispers never leave,
That part is clear
Maybe it's denial,
My own deep-rooted fear

And if I must go, why shouldn't I?
Accept their comfort on the way?

No, I do not deserve to die this way

But that's not what they say

Meaghan Stout
Lincoln, Nebraska

Villa

The cricket orchestra's begun
  Its symphony of unrelieved
Long stilted…What's that, "chirps"?…born of
  The setting Sun,

With imitative chirpchirp frogs
  And their— monotonous— and not
Conclusive— line; so nature goes.
  The evening's hot,

The guests who move across the lawn
  Are overdressed, the female thighs
Push stiff brocaded gowns along
  The grass. Burn, eyes:

Such jewels around their necks! And on
  Their chests, below the ears, with one
Piece drilled into a nose, and on
  Their wrists. The men?

Those collars stiff, their jackets black—
  All crows. But these are *major* men,
The beauty of their younger wives
  Tells that. Their lives

Are brief as insects', but they think
  They own the stars above.
                    Go on?
But why? Below the stars they think
  They own the sky.

                    Go on? The Earth,
The seas, the bodies and the rest.

Ira Rosenstein
Astoria, New York

Downbeats

By day he worked on teeth
by night he built ships in bottles
lured into small speechless places
he picked at precision
aimed tweezers at irregularities
under his fixed bright light
he played barely audible
jazz in the background
discordant crying moans blues
with ragtime gypsy spirit moves
sudden and unexpected pokes of sound
to keep him afloat in his sea of spittle
safe behind his mask
glorying in the confines
but ready to take off
without a moment's notice

Susan Shea
Milford, Pennsylvania

The Hedgehog

There is a hedgehog stuck inside me
I can't remember eating it
the spines
all seven thousand of them
prick me at once sometimes
and my whole body tenses up
alone, I have no defence
in the past, I numbed the pain
but it's rude to ignore the hedgehog and we ought to
    communicate
doesn't mean to attack
its spines are vulnerability
I would tell it to leave
I've tried this and it doesn't work
the hedgehog has lived here for years
it has something to say to me.

Poppy Hulbert
Farnham, England, UK

Choices with Attributes of Self

When it didn't know choosing, it chose
a scruff field, a sapling tree, breaking clovers
on small tin plates offered to the clouds;

chose setting out on bike wheels
to a library, park pond, leading friends
along pencil-thin walkways;

chose Nancy Drew's blue roadster
that could go anywhere, searching down clues;
chose outwardly to follow rules and schedules

inwardly, to fall away from time;
chose Lincoln, Robert Louis Stevenson, Thoreau
by heart and by curriculum, Robert Frost by love,

and a teacher-poet in Hartford who spoke
poet to poet to a child; chose stars in tangled branches
and a gold-spangled dancer

the very undulating path itself the moon threw
on the dark waters of the Sound; chose
depths in one lover over a lifetime;

chose honoring a family
that made a first universe contain her
which grew to a second, a third and to a passing cloud—

chose to forgive the choices of other choosers;
chose to venture inwards for more dreams
for the better parts of countless succeed-fails;

chose coming to impasse, giving up to pursue passion
circling in on itself to the succeed-fails;
began again, choosing a pen, a brush, a set of keys;

chose rebirth, wild hair, lyric-
jumps, piano tears. Chose
"Let's see what we've got in here" (Dad

crawling in behind to repair the TV);
chose a free walk in the open air, postcards
from the backyard, and always

more love, more love, more love
and more life, the kind that goes out
unwavering in brave eyes

Marilyn E. Johnston
Bloomfield, Connecticut

Severance

My mother ties a rope around my feet
so I won't knock her in my sleep
only I don't sleep.

When war is over I return. Her mother's face
is now her face. She serves the food
asks if it tastes like I remember.

Niki Orfanou
London, UK

Incident in the Suburbs

What dark force drives the mole
to tunnel through my lawn
like a cat under a bedsheet?
He churns it up
in a faintly zigzag pattern
from the sidewalk to the flower bed.
I hate his purblind fervor
and its raised brown trail
across my weedy sward.
Castor oil. Nematodes. Will nothing stop
his infernal digging? I want to steer him
across the street into my neighbor's yard.
Under cover of night of course.
With no trace back to me.

Rich Rohdenburg
Duluth, Georgia

Certain Women

Instead of a woman, he called you gorgeous.

Loudly he said to his wife, See?

I don't just say it about women. Both his wife and their friend

were a little butch. Your new glasses

were really something else. A terminal degree

in Critical Studies who made friends with a fog bank.

A hunk of brass carved back to its true form.

His shirt, striped and stiff, strained over his intestines.

You said there was clearly a cost to certainty.

In trying to understand you, I said certainty is utterly

vulnerable. Mr. Sheffield, wouldn't you say?

There's nothing worse than making plain what you want.

All summer I cultivated a thick skin of dead cells.

Psychically, many infestations.

Daytime, we thrifted costumes and schlepped our kits

in uncut upstate fields and nightly sat drunk on the laps

of local meth addicts at an aesthetically misguided

abolition-era gay bar that closed before Walmart did.

Is there anything worse than someone

who doesn't seem to know any better than you do insisting

your painful and likely fruitless body slams against a pane

of glass will lead to anything? How would they know?

Your spit and blood are Pollocked on the pane.

And if they know, then you've finally found kin to god:

a lithe young man with a husband teaching at Oxford.

See? I don't just think. I throw myself.

Valentine Freeman
Los Osos, California

Blackbird

for Steve

A blackbird circles above me in cloud-filled skies
over the piney woods, the cornfields green and stubbled with
    new growth.
I witness the rise of a blackbird on wing carrying a prophesy: an
    omen.
New love will arrive this season.
The creature soaring calls to me:
"Beware!" it calls "Beware!"

I want to capture the freedom of its flight,
over the houses, the avenues, the church roofs.
A kind of freedom I have never known.

A shred of black paper against a cardboard-colored sky—
a blackbird warbles, spreads its wings, and sings.
What do we now know of love?

This is a lyric in which I give thanks
for what is known: the fever you give me,
and gratitude for all the joy,
for you solo to my soul.

Beth Brown Preston
West Chester, Pennsylvania

Herbert Hoover Library

It's right off I-80 in Iowa,
a complex covering several acres like
a golf course, with a clapboard village and

a one-room school house along gravel paths,
but the library is standard brick and glass,
low-slung with a sleek asphalt parking lot;

inside, we learn that Hoover used to be
a top-of-the-line mining engineer,
academic, and administrator

before entering politics to become
the scapegoat Great Depression president,
which is all that people remember now.

Half the scattered cars in the main lot
have out-of-state plates, so Hoover draws
a few tourists, if not whole buses full,

generating local employment
not tied to hog confinements or corn farms,
so he's the default local hero there

and lynchpin of a cottage industry,
although the plaques say he left as a child
and never came back while he was alive.

David Stephenson
Detroit, Michigan

Dorothy and Me

The movie, when I first saw it,
was a little scary …

but I did like Dorothy—how she was kind,
helped others, ventured to new places,
never gave up—and I love that
Over the Rainbow song—don't you?

Oh yes—I know about Dorothy,
about farm life, about dogs, too—
though I never had one named Toto,
and I don't know much about ruby slippers.

But I know about tornadoes—
like the one that came barreling
toward our Kansas farmhouse, striking
terror in my 5-year-old heart before
it swerved at the last minute and
destroyed a neighbor's barn instead.

And maybe I've been to Oz—
at least it felt like it on my first trip out of
Kansas when I was fourteen, to California
and back in a 2-door sedan, seeing mountains,
deserts, and an ocean for the first time.

Like Dorothy, I've had adventures on
a few yellow-brick-roads in my life, but
I've never seen a witch or a wizard—
although I did once see a real prince.

And, like Dorothy, I eventually found
my way home, though *home* was
not in Kansas anymore.

Carmen Ward
Durham, North Carolina